In The
Upper Room

A Drama For Maundy Thursday

GEORGIANNA SUMMERS

CSS Publishing Company, Inc.
Lima, Ohio

IN THE UPPER ROOM

ISBN: 0-7880-0725-4

Staging Directions

This drama can be presented either in a church sanctuary or a social hall. There are no parts to be memorized. Most of the reading is done out of sight, and the acting is done in pantomime. However, it should be carefully rehearsed so that the acting and the narration coincide.

At the beginning, Sophia, the Greek woman, should stand in front of the audience either at a pulpit, lectern, or speaker's stand where she can lay her script. She later joins Mark and John to continue reading the script out of sight. She should be in a simple Greek costume. Jesus and the disciples should be in biblical costumes.

The stage setting should include two areas — one for the footwashing and the other for the meal. There should be a basin, a towel, a pitcher of warm water, and a low bench or stool in the footwashing area. The table for the meal should have 13 chairs or stools arranged along one side facing the audience and at each end. Two chalices, a loaf of French bread, and a pitcher of wine or grape juice should be in the center at Jesus' place. A small goblet should be at each disciple's place along with a small bowl for every three people. Candles should be placed along the table or a menorah in the center.

When Peter and John enter, John should carry a basket with a container of haroseth (the apple, cinnamon, and nut mix that is part of the Seder meal) or applesauce, a tablespoon, and several small baskets of uncooked flour tortillas. In preparing the table he can put the baskets of tortillas along the table (for the disciples to tear off and dip into the haroseth) and spoon the haroseth into the small bowls. While he is doing this, Peter can light the candles and pour a small amount of wine or grape juice into each of the small goblets.

The footwashing scene should be carefully rehearsed so that the entrance and footwashing of each disciple coincides with

5

the information about the disciple in the script. This will help the audience have a clear picture of who each disciple is. Disciples who enter together can gesture and pantomime talking to each other or greeting others who are already on stage. Some can show surprise at Jesus' taking the servant role. The zealots can be involved in heated conversation, gesturing with clenched fists. As the footwashing progresses, small clusters of three or four disciples can be formed in unobtrusive areas of the staging area away from the center where they can pantomime visiting with each other.

For the communion sharing, Jesus breaks the loaf of bread, tears off a piece, then sends half the loaf down the table to his right, the other half to his left. After each disciple has broken off a piece he pours the wine or grape juice from the pitcher into each chalice before him, dips his bread into one and partakes, then sends a chalice to his right and one to his left. After the disciples have all partaken, the ones on each end take the bread to the audience, then return and take the chalices. (If the congregation is small, one chalice will do.)

During the narration after the communion the disciples can pass the tortillas to each other and use them to dip into the haroseth. They should be drinking and using the dip throughout the meal and pantomime talking to each other to give action to the drama when no specific action is called for in the narration.

Source Material

Barclay, William. *The Gospel of John. Daily Study Bible Series, Vols. 1 and 2. Revised Editions.* Philadelphia: Westminster Press, 1975.

The Gospel of Mark. Daily Study Bible Series. Revised Edition. Philadelphia: Westminster Press, 1975.

The Master's Men. Nashville: Abingdon Press, 1983.

In The Upper Room

(The service may begin with a call to worship, hymn, prayer, and so forth. Following this, SOPHIA, dressed in costume, enters and reads from the pulpit, lectern, or speaker's stand.)

Sophia: My name is Sophia. I am a citizen of Ephesus, where there is a large Christian community here at the beginning of the second century after the birth of Christ. This church was founded by a missionary named Paul about 50 years ago, and I have been drawn to it by the kind of people who are in it — how they care for each other and for the world. So I have come seeking to know more about this Jesus whom they follow and the God that he made known by his life and death. However, before I can be baptized and received into this faith I must first receive instruction because, being Greek, I know very little about the history and the beliefs and practices of this religion.

I am fortunate in my instructors. They are two elderly men who knew those first disciples of Jesus personally. One of them is John Mark. He grew up in Jerusalem, and his mother was a believer in Jesus. After Jesus' death and resurrection appearances, the disciples, along with Jesus' mother and brothers, met in her home; so John Mark got to know them well, especially Peter. When he became a teenager he went with his uncle, Barnabas, and the apostle Paul on their first missionary journey to Cyprus. Later he went to Rome, where Paul was imprisoned, to help him. But most importantly, about 30 years ago he wrote a biography of Jesus, the first one to be written. He got most of his information from Peter so it's firsthand material from someone who was actually there with Jesus and knew all the things that happened.

My other instructor is a man named John the Elder. He got his information from another disciple — John. John was the youngest disciple, and Jesus loved him dearly. He lived to be very old here in Ephesus, and the church here encouraged him to record his remembrances. John the Elder wrote them down so we have another book about Jesus by these two men. It's very different from Mark's, I suppose because Peter and John were very different. Peter was blunt and matter-of-fact. He just told it like it was, just the facts. John was more reflective. He was interested in the spiritual and symbolic meaning of Jesus' actions and words, and since he lived so long he had a lifetime to reflect on his experiences with Jesus and their meaning. So he didn't tell it to John the Elder like a biography in chronological order from birth to death but more like an old man's remembrances of important events and what Jesus was revealing about himself and God through them.

Both of these men have made Jesus and his disciples very real to me and because they have written it down, future generations will find this to be true for them as well. Tonight they are going to tell me about the last meal Jesus had with his disciples because the remembrance of this is an important weekly celebration in the church. I invite you to come with me now and listen to these two tell the story as they heard it from Peter and John. They will make it real for you, too. *(She moves out of sight to join MARK and JOHN.)* off stage

Mark: On the first day of the Festival of Unleavened Bread, the day the lambs for the Passover meal were killed, Jesus' disciples asked him, "Where do you want us to go and get the Passover meal ready for you?" Then Jesus sent two of them with these instructions: "Go into the city, and a man carrying a jar of water will meet you. Follow him to the house he enters, and say to the owner of the house: 'The Teacher says, "Where is the room where my disciples and I will eat the Passover meal?" ' Then he will show you a large upstairs room, fixed up and furnished, where you will get everything ready for us." The disciples left, went to the city, and found everything just as Jesus had told them; and they prepared the Passover meal. (Mark 14:12-16 TEV)

(PETER and JOHN enter and finish preparing the table. See Staging Directions.)

Sophia: Who were the two disciples he sent?

Mark: Peter and John.

Sophia: Tell me about them.

Mark: Peter was a natural leader, a real extrovert. He was usually the first to speak up, blurting out what he thought and then wishing he hadn't. He often had to eat his words. His real name was Simon, but Jesus called him Peter, which means rock, because he saw strong, rock-like traits in him underneath all his bravado. He was emotional, quick-tempered, impulsive — and likeable, a very warm man.

John: And a man of action — again sometimes without thinking first.

Sophia: And John?

John: I only knew him in his later years, but Mark tells me that when he was young he and his brother James were very hot-tempered. The sons of thunder Jesus called them. He and James were first cousins of Jesus. Their mother Salome was a sister of Mary, Jesus' mother. This may be why they and Peter were the ones he chose to be closest to him.

Mark: Very likely. And Jesus especially loved John. He was the youngest, and I think Jesus wanted to encourage him and help him harness his hot temper, which he did.

John: Yes. When I knew him in his old age he was all love.

Mark: Anyway, he and Peter prepared the meal, and when evening came Jesus and the others arrived. *(JESUS comes in, followed by JAMES.)* That's Jesus there and James with him. *(JESUS greets JOHN and PETER and motions for them to come to him to wash their feet. PETER hangs back while JOHN and JAMES take off their sandals and JESUS starts to wash JAMES' feet.)*

Sophia: Was James anything like his brother?

John: Not really, except he had a temper, too. There was that incident about the Samaritan village that rejected them. They both wanted to destroy it. James was older than John and was usually with him, perhaps to look after him. He was very loyal to Jesus and didn't seem to have any jealousy about John's being the favorite. He was the first disciple to be martyred for his faith. He was beheaded by Herod.

Sophia: How terrible.

Mark: It is not easy to be a Christian, Sophia. That's why you must be very sure that you want to be one of us.

Sophia: Why is Jesus washing their feet?

Mark: The roads in Palestine were very dusty; so a gracious host always had a servant wash his guests' feet when they entered his house after traveling.

John: But you will notice, Sophia, that Jesus is doing the servant's job. John told me this. It was a vivid memory. *(JESUS motions for PETER to take his sandals off and PETER shakes his head.)* When he came to Peter, Peter blurted out, "Never at any time will you wash *my* feet!"

Sophia: Why?

Mark: I told you that Peter always talked first and thought later.

10

John: Peter loved Jesus, and I think he was embarrassed that Jesus had taken the servant role. But Jesus said, "If I do not wash your feet, you will no longer be my disciple."

Mark: And wonderful impulsive Peter said, "Lord, do not wash only my feet, then. Wash my hands and head, too!" *(JESUS shakes his head and washes PETER's feet.)* He certainly didn't want to be crossed off the disciple list. *(ANDREW enters.)* Here comes Andrew now.

Sophia: Who was he?

John: He was Peter's brother.

Sophia: Was he as impulsive as Peter?

Mark: No, he was very quiet and unassuming. Just like James he didn't seem to mind taking second place to his brother — never begrudged the fact that he was not one of the inner circle.

John: We could use a few more like him in the church. He was always bringing people to Jesus. In fact, he was the one who introduced Peter to Jesus.

Mark: All four of these men were fishermen from Bethsaida on the Sea of Galilee. They left a thriving business to follow Jesus. *(PHILIP and NATHANAEL come in.)* And here comes someone else from Bethsaida — Philip. As usual he has his friend Nathanael with him.

John: It seems to me that Philip was somewhat of a pessimist. Remember at the feeding of the 5,000 Jesus asked him, "Where can we buy enough food to feed all these people?" And his answer was, "For everyone to have even a little, it would take more than 200 silver coins to buy enough bread." He was like a lot of people in the church who say, "It would be nice to do it, but it can't be done."

11

Mark: Well, he was a practical man. He had a hard time believing in the power of the unseen.

John: That's true. Here at the last supper he asked Jesus to show him the Father, and he didn't understand that they had been seeing God all along in Jesus.

Mark: But before we are too hard on him, remember that he wanted to share Christ with others. As soon as he was called, he looked up his friend Nathanael Bartholomew there and invited him to meet Jesus.

John: Nathanael was reluctant at first. He was from Cana, which was a rival village of Nazareth; so he made an offhand joke about it — "Can anything good come from Nazareth?" Philip didn't argue. He just said, "Come and see." And Nathanael did.

Sophia: What kind of person was *he*?

John: A sincerely devout man. Even before Philip had invited him, Jesus had observed him sitting under the fig tree in front of his house and recognized that he was very sincere about his faith.

Sophia: How could Jesus tell that just by seeing him under a fig tree when he hadn't even met him?

Mark: Because, Sophia, the houses of poorer people had only one room, but almost everyone had a tall and widespread fig tree in front of their house, which they used as a place of privacy and prayer. He was probably praying or studying the scriptures, and Jesus observed him without his knowing it.

John: I think you're right. We know that both Philip and Nathanael had been seriously studying the scriptures trying to discover who the Messiah might be because Philip told

Nathanael, "We have found the one whom Moses wrote about in the book of the Law and whom the prophets also wrote about." Nathanael really believed Jesus was the Messiah. *(THOMAS enters.)*

Mark: Here comes Thomas. If Nathanael was an instant believer, Thomas was just the opposite. He had to have proof.

John: Yes, he was the questioner. Again here at this last meal when Jesus said, "You know the way that leads to the place where I am going," Thomas' response was, "Lord, we *don't* know where you are going, so how can we know the way to get there?" Like Philip he was very down-to-earth and honest about his doubts.

Mark: And he had to have proof that Jesus had been raised from the dead.

John: Right. He wasn't with the others when Jesus appeared to them, and he thought they were just imagining it. Said he wouldn't believe it unless he could put his finger on the nail scars in Jesus' hands and his hand on the wound in his side.

Mark: But when Jesus appeared to him and let him do this, he believed wholeheartedly. I like Thomas. He was a thinker, and through his questions and honest doubts he came to a strong faith that was his own rather than a weak, uncommitted one based on others' beliefs. *(MATTHEW and JAMES, the sons of Alphaeus, enter.)*

Sophia: Who are these two men?

John: They are two more brothers — Matthew or Levi and James, both sons of Alphaeus.

Sophia: They don't look anything like brothers. Matthew looks like a wealthy businessman, and James looks — well, I'm not sure I'd want to be in the same room with *him.*

Mark: *(Laughing)* You've hit it right, Sophia. Matthew was a tax collector and very wealthy.

John: Also very hated by his fellow Jews and very lonely. The only friends he had were other tax collectors.

Sophia: Then how did he come to know Jesus?

Mark: He conducted his business at the seat of customs at Capernaum by the seashore where Jesus preached. Jesus had a lot to say about the dangers of laying up earthly treasures for yourself and that must have touched Matthew's heart. When Jesus called him, he gave up his position and followed him.

John: He also invited other tax collectors to his home to meet Jesus, which got Jesus into a lot of trouble with the Pharisees.

Sophia: What about his brother James? He looks dangerous.

Mark: He was a zealot, *(SIMON and THADDAEUS enter and stand to one side)* like those other two who have just come in. Zealots were extremely patriotic Jews who wanted to overthrow the Romans by violence. James must have hated Matthew for collaborating with the enemy. But here they are reconciled to each other under the spirit of Jesus. That can happen in families, you know.

Sophia: How did Jesus come to include zealots among his disciples since he was so opposed to violence?

John: That's probably why. He wanted to show them a better way to deal with enemies — God's way. He knew that violence only leads to more violence.

Sophia: Did they get his message?

14

John: It was hard for them, impossible for one of them. *(JU-DAS enters and stands to one side by himself.)* You see, Sophia, there were different ideas about the kind of person the Messiah would be. Some of the Jewish scriptures said he would be a military and political leader like King David. Most Jews believed this and certainly the zealots did. That's why these last four who have come in were attracted to Jesus. They thought he would be this kind of Messiah.

Sophia: Who were these last three who have come in?

Mark: The first is Simon who is always designated as Simon the zealot. He obviously was not quiet about his convictions. Next to him is a man named Judas Thaddaeus. I like to call him by his second name so we don't confuse him with Judas Iscariot.

John: You were asking, Sophia, if these zealots understood Jesus' message of nonviolence? Even here at this last meal with Jesus they were still hoping he would be a military leader who would rally all the Jews to rise up and overthrow the Romans. Thaddaeus here asked him why he wouldn't show his power and reveal himself to the world and not just to them.

Sophia: What did Jesus say?

John: He tried to tell Thaddaeus and all the disciples that his power came from God and that God's power is revealed through love not force. He pleaded with them to obey his teaching if they truly loved him.

Sophia: How could they possibly *not* understand him?

Mark: We are all such slow learners, Sophia. Like Philip and Thomas and these super-patriotic Jews, we find it easy to trust the power of human beings which we can see and hard to trust the power of God which we often cannot see.

Sophia: But they *could* see it in Jesus. He was right there with them demonstrating it.

John: Yes, and he was to demonstrate it even further, as you will see.

Sophia: This last man standing alone. Who is he?

Mark: He is all of us. His name is Judas Iscariot, meaning "Man of Kerioth," a place in Judah in the south of Palestine. He is the only disciple who is not from Galilee in the north. He stands alone partly because he senses he is an outsider.

Sophia: Doesn't he relate to the other zealots? You *did* say these last four who came in were zealots.

Mark: Yes, that's his connection with the group, probably why he joined. He was looking for a leader to overthrow the Romans and thought he had found him in Jesus.

Sophia: Why did Jesus include him? Surely he must have known what his expectations were.

John: I think Jesus saw other possibilities in him and hoped to draw those out. He may have admired Judas' concern for his fellow Jews suffering under the Roman yoke and hoped to show him a better way than insurrection to help his people. He gave him the responsibility of being treasurer of the group; so he must have affirmed him as an honest person who could be trusted with other people's money.

Sophia: And *was* he trustworthy?

Mark: John didn't think he was. He called him a thief; so he obviously didn't trust him. I don't really know, but I do think there was little joy in him and criticism of those who didn't agree with him. But let's move on with the story.

16

John: After Jesus had washed their feet, he asked, "Do you understand what I have just done to you? I, your Lord and Teacher, have just washed your feet. You, then, should wash one another's feet. I have set an example for you so that you will do just what I have done for you."

(The DISCIPLES and JESUS move to the table. JAMES and JOHN move to sit on JESUS' left and right, but JESUS motions for JUDAS to sit on his left. JUDAS is surprised and pantomimes, "You want me?" JESUS nods and JAMES moves down.)

Mark: As they moved to the table James and John may have assumed they would sit on the right and left of Jesus. They had asked for this special privilege before, which had made the other disciples angry, and Jesus had used that incident to teach all the disciples a much-needed lesson about greatness and servanthood. On this occasion he kept John on his right hand, but he invited Judas to sit at his left. This was the seat of honor at all Jewish banquets.

Sophia: Why did he put *Judas* there? I would have thought he would have chosen Peter or anybody besides Judas.

Mark: Remember I said that Judas saw himself as an outsider. I think Jesus wanted so much for him to feel a part of the group. Jesus always reached out to include the outcasts, and on this particular night Judas was very much on his heart because he knew Judas' intentions.

John: Yes. While they were at supper Jesus said, "I have wanted so much to eat this Passover meal with you before I suffer."

Mark: Then he took a piece of bread, gave a prayer of thanks, broke it, and gave it to his disciples. "Take it," he said. "This is my body broken for you. Do this in memory of me." Then he took a cup, gave thanks to God, and handed it to them; and they all drank from it. Jesus said, "This is my blood which is poured out for many; my blood which seals God's covenant.

17

Whenever you drink it, do so in memory of me." *(The DIS-CIPLES partake of the communion; then the ones on each end take it to the congregation. They then return to the table.)*

John: After Jesus had shared the bread and the cup, he was deeply troubled and declared openly, "I am telling you the truth. One of you is going to betray me."

Mark: The disciples were upset and began to ask him, one after the other, "Surely you don't mean me, do you?"

John: Peter motioned to John who was sitting next to Jesus and said, "Ask him whom he is talking about." So the disciple moved closer to Jesus' side and asked, "Who is it, Lord?" Jesus answered, "I will dip some bread in the sauce and give it to him; he is the man." So he took a piece of bread, dipped it, and gave it to Judas on his left and said to him privately, "Hurry, and do what you must!" None of the others at the table understood why Jesus said this to him. Since Judas was in charge of the money bag, some of the disciples thought that Jesus had told him to go and buy what they needed for the festival, or to give something to the poor. Judas accepted the bread and went out at once. It was night. *(JUDAS leaves.)*

Sophia: What was he planning to do?

Mark: He had already made arrangements with the chief priests to hand Jesus over to them at night when no one was around to protest, and they promised him money. Judas knew Jesus would be going to the garden of Gethsemane nearby to pray after the meal and that this would be a good place to take him.

Sophia: But *why?* Jesus was his friend. Why would he betray him?

Mark: I don't think he saw it as betrayal. He was so obsessed with his desire to get rid of the Romans that he wanted to

18

force Jesus to use his power. I think he believed that this confrontation would cause Jesus to become his kind of Messiah, that even the angels of God would descend to help him and all Jerusalem would then rise up to support him and overthrow the Romans. He was wrong, of course, and when he saw his dream turn to ashes and realized how he had been used and what he had done to his friend, he couldn't live with himself. He took the money back to the priests and went out and hanged himself.

Sophia: What a tragic man! *(Pause)* But I don't understand, Mark, why you said earlier that Judas is all of us. In what way?

Mark: Because he refused to accept Jesus for who he was and tried to make him into what he wanted him to be. Jesus knew that God's way was not the way of force — and so do we. But most of the time we are afraid to trust the power of love and instead rely on might.

John: And often justify it in the name of Christ. We forget what John told me that Jesus said here at this meal. "My commandment is this: love one another, just as I love you. The greatest love a person can have for his friends is to give his life for them. And you are my friends if you do what I command you — love one another. And now, peace I leave with you, my peace I give to you. *(Pause)* Come now, let us go from this place."

(The DISCIPLES and JESUS get up and leave quietly. The audience may do the same or the service may be concluded with a hymn, an appropriate anthem or solo, or a prayer.)